HAYES PRESS
ISBN 1-871126-09-6

SUNSHINE IN THE VALLEY

HAYES PRESS
ISBN 1-871126-09-6

Introduction

The promises of God are very precious and there is nothing to equal the rays of sunshine from His word to warm the cold days of doubt and despair.

This daily devotional has been carefully and prayerfully prepared to give help in this direction. It can be read for personal enjoyment and blessing, or to those who are aged, lonely, needy, bedridden, or sick. It is the pure word of God, a living thing in a dying world.

May God bless abundantly its distribution!

Reg Darke

Day One

Protection

This I will know that God is for me. [1]

The Lord is with me; He is my helper. [2]

If God is for us, who can be against us? [3]

So we say with confidence,
  The Lord is my helper; I will not be afraid.
  What can man do to me? [4]

The soul that on Jesus hath leaned for repose,
I will not, I cannot desert to its foes;
That soul, though all hell should endeavour to shake,
I'll never, no never, no never forsake.

---

[1]*Psalm 56:9* [2]*Psalm 118:7* [3]*Romans 8:31*
[4]*Hebrews 13:6*

Day Two

Trust

———————

Trust in the Lord and do good [1]

*Delight yourself in the Lord
and he will give you the desires of your heart.* [2]

*Commit your way to the Lord;
trust in him and he will do this.* [3]

*Be still before the Lord
and wait patiently for him.* [4]

Wait for the Lord and keep his way. [5]

> **In all thy joys and blessings,
> His hand has its full share;
> Whilst oft-times in thy sorrow,
> His purposes lie there.**

———————

[1]*Psalm 37:3*   [2]*Psalm 37:4*   [3]*Psalm 37:5*
[4]*Psalm 37:7*   [5]*Psalm 37:34*

Day Three

Guidance

The Lord will guide you always;
He will satisfy your needs in a sun-scorched land. [1]

But when He, the Spirit of Truth, comes,
He will guide you into all truth. [2]

To guide our feet into the path of peace. [3]

You guide me with your counsel,
and afterwards you will take me into glory. [4]

Guide us, O Thou great Jehovah,
Pilgrims through this barren land;
We are weak, but Thou art mighty,
Hold us with Thy powerful hand;
Bread of heaven!
Feed us now and evermore.

---

[1] Isaiah 58:11   [2] John 16:13   [3] Luke 1:79
[4] Psalm 73:24

Day Four

Love

_____

*I have loved you with an everlasting love;
I have drawn you with loving-kindness.* [1]

Love covers over a multitude of sins. [2]

Love covers over all wrongs. [3]

The Son of God who loved me and gave himself for me. [4]

**And when I think that God, His Son not sparing,
Sent Him to die, I scarce can take it in.
That on the Cross, my burden gladly bearing,
He bled and died, to take away my sin.
How great Thou art.**

_____

[1] Jeremiah 31:3   [2] 1 Peter 4:8   [3] Proverbs 10:12
[4] Galatians 2:20

Day Five

Blessing

Blessed is he whose transgressions are forgiven,
 Whose sins are covered. [1]

Blessed is the man who trusts in you. [2]

Blessed are those whose strength is in you,
 Who have set their hearts on pilgrimage. [3]

Blessed are those who dwell in your house;
 they are ever praising you. [4]

Happy they who trust in Jesus;
Sweet their portion is and sure,
While the foe on others seizes,
He will keep His own secure.
Happy people!
Happy though despised and poor.

---

[1] *Psalm 32:1*   [2] *Psalm 84:12*   [3] *Psalm 84:5*
 [4] *Psalm 84:4*

Day Six

Cheer

Be of good cheer... thy sins be forgiven thee. [1]

Be of good cheer! I have overcome the world. [2]

Be of good cheer! It is I; be not afraid. [3]

Be of good cheer, for I believe God, that it shall be even as it was told me. [4]

Now I exhort you to be of good cheer. [5]

> **Rejoice and be glad!**
> **For the Lord is on high;**
> **Christ pleadeth for us**
> **On God's throne in the sky.**

---

[1] Matthew 9:2 (AV) [2] John 16:33 (AV)
[3] Matthew 14:27 (AV)
[4] Acts 27:25 (AV) [5] Acts 27:22 (AV)

Day Seven

Forgiveness

I, even I, am he who blots out your transgressions, for my own sake, and remembers your sins no more. [1]

Who is God like you, who pardons sin and forgives the transgression of the remnant of his inheritance? [2]

You will tread our sins underfoot and hurl all our iniquities into the depths of the sea. [3]

Jesus said… Your sins are forgiven. [4]

**We bless Jehovah's Name,
Our sins are all forgiven.
To suffer once to earth Christ came,
And now He's crowned in heaven.**

---

[1] Isaiah 43:25 [2] Micah 7:18 [3] Micah 7:19
[4] Luke 7:48

Day Eight

Peace

Jesus said... Your faith has saved you;
go in peace.¹

Peace I leave with you; my peace I give you.
I do not give to you as the world gives.²

For God was pleased... through him to reconcile
to himself all things... making peace through
his blood, shed on the cross. ³

For he himself is our peace ⁴

When peace, like a river, attendeth my way,
When sorrows, like sea-billows, roll;
Whatever my lot, Thou has taught me to say,
"It is well, it is well with my soul".

---

¹Luke 7:50 ²John 14:27 ³Colossians 1:19,20
⁴Ephesians 2:14

Day Nine

Seeking

Reach out for him and find him. [1]

If only I knew where to find him. [2]

He is not far from each one of us.
   For in him we live and move and have our being. [3]

Without faith it is impossible to please God, because anyone who comes to him must believe that he exists and that he rewards those who earnestly seek him. [4]

So I say to you… seek and you will find. [5]

> **Days are filled with sorrow and care,**
> **Hearts are lonely and drear;**
> **Burdens are lifted at Calvary,**
> **Jesus is very near.**

---

[1]*Acts 17:27* [2]*Job 23:3*
[3]*Acts 17:27,28* [4]*Hebrews 11:6*
[5]*Luke 11:9*

Day Ten

Provision

My God will meet all your needs according to his glorious riches in Christ Jesus. [1]

My God is my rock, in whom I take refuge. [2]

My God sent his angel, and he shut the mouths of the lions. They have not hurt me. [3]

He is my God, and I will praise him. [4]

**My God, I am Thine,
What a comfort Divine!
What a blessing to know that
Christ Jesus is mine!**

---

[1] Philippians 4:19 [2] Psalm 18:2
[3] Daniel 6:22 [4] Exodus 15:2

Day Eleven

Deliverance

I have no refuge; no-one cares for my life. [1]

For the Son of Man came to seek and to save what was lost. [2]

In your love you kept me from the pit of destruction. [3]

The Lord will save me. [4]

I do believe; help me overcome my unbelief! [5]

> **From sinking sand He lifted me,**
> **With tender hand, He lifted me.**
> **From shades of night to plains of light,**
> **Oh, praise His name, He lifted me.**

---

[1] Psalm 142:4 [2] Luke 19:10 [3] Isaiah 38:17
[4] Isaiah 38:20 [5] Mark 9:24

Day Twelve

Standing Still

Fear ye not. Stand still, and see the salvation of the Lord. [1]

But stand thou still a while, that I may shew thee the word of God. [2]

Now therefore stand still, that I may reason with you before the Lord of all the righteous acts of the Lord. [3]

Stand still and consider the wondrous works of God. [4]

> **Stand and adore! How glorious He**
> **That dwells in bright eternity;**
> **We gaze and we confound our sight,**
> **Plunged in the abyss of dazzling light.**

---

[1] Exodus 14:13 (AV) [2] 1 Samuel 9:27 (AV)
[3] 1 Samuel 12:7 (AV) [4] Job 37:14 (AV)

Day Thirteen

The Tree

Moses cried unto the Lord, and the Lord showed him a tree. [1]

Jesus... whom you had killed by hanging him on a tree. [2]

Just as Moses lifted up the snake in the desert, so the Son of Man must be lifted up. [3]

Turn to me and be saved, all you ends of the earth; for I am God, and there is no other. [4]

**As we survey the wondrous cross
On which the Lord of glory died,
Our richest gains we count but loss,
And pour contempt on all our pride.**

---

[1] Exodus 15:25(AV) [2] Acts 5:30 [3] John 3:14 [4] Isaiah 45:22

Day Fourteen

Our Leader

And the Lord went before them by day in a pillar of a cloud to lead them the way. [1]

For the sake of your name lead and guide me. [2]

Lead me in a straight path. [3]

This is how you guided your people to make for yourself a glorious name. [4]

**Grant us at least one step to see,
Marked out for us by Thy decree;
If now Thou wilt not give more light,
Help us to take this one step right.**

---

[1]*Exodus 13:21(AV)* [2]*Psalm 31:3* [3]*Psalm 27:11*
[4]*Isaiah 63:14*

Day Fifteen

Treasure

The Almighty will be your gold, the choicest silver for you. [1]

Provide purses for yourselves that will not wear out, a treasure in heaven that will not be exhausted.[2]

For where your treasure is, there your heart will be also.[3]

Has not God chosen those who are poor in the eyes of the world to be rich in faith and to inherit the kingdom.[4]

**But of all the wealth of bliss,
Which Christ's poorness brought us,
We shall treasure none like this,
'Twas Himself that bought us.**

---

[1] Job 22:25   [2] Luke 12:33   [3] Luke 12:34
[4] James 2:5

Day Sixteen

Following

Make level paths for your feet and take only ways that are firm. Do not swerve to the right or the left; keep your foot from evil. [1]

Direct my footsteps according to your word; let no sin rule over me. [2]

My steps have held to your paths; my feet have not slipped. [3]

Follow me. [4]

**Lead Thou us on while here below,
From step to step Thy guidance show;
Till Christ for us shall come again
And take us home. Come, Lord, Amen.**

---

[1]*Proverbs 4:26, 27* [2]*Psalm 119:133* [3]*Psalm 17:5*
[4]*John 21:22*

Day Seventeen

The Rock

There is no Rock like our God. [1]

Lead me to the rock that is higher than I. [2]

The Lord said, There is a place near me where you may stand on a rock. [3]

I will put you in a cleft in the rock and cover you with my hand. [4]

Trust thou in God, He is a rock, a tower;
Trust thou in God, thy stronghold is His power;
Trust thou in God, His promises are sure;
Trust thou in God, in Him thou art secure.

---

[1] 1 Samuel 2:2   [2] Psalm 61:2   [3] Exodus 33:21
[4] Exodus 33:22

Day Eighteen

Grace and mercy

You are forgiving and good O Lord, abounding in love to all who call to you. [1]

For you are great and do marvellous deeds; you alone are God. [2]

But Thou, O Lord, art a God full of compassion and gracious, longsuffering, and plenteous in mercy and truth . [3]

**Great God of wonders, all Thy ways
Are worthy of Thyself, divine,
But the bright glories of Thy grace
Beyond Thine other wonders shine.
Who is a pardoning God like Thee,
Or who hath grace so rich and free?**

---

[1]*Psalm 86:5* [2]*Psalm 86:10* [3]*Psalm 86:15 (AV)*

Day Nineteen

Humility

Should you then seek great things for yourself? Seek them not. [1]

I live in a high and holy place, but also with him who is contrite and lowly in spirit, to revive the spirit of the lowly and to revive the heart of the contrite. [2]

God opposes the proud but gives grace to the humble. Humble yourselves, therefore, under God's mighty hand, that He may lift you up in due time. [3]

For I am gentle and humble in heart. [4]

**My highest place is lying low
At my Redeemer's feet;
No higher joy in life I know,
Than in His service sweet.**

---

[1] Jeremiah 45:5 [2] Isaiah 57:15 [3] 1 Peter 5:5, 6
[4] Matthew 11:29

Day twenty

Waiting in Hope

———————

*But now, Lord, what do I look for?
My hope is in you.* [1]

No-one whose hope is in you will ever be put to shame. [2]

Wait for the Lord; be strong and take heart and wait for the Lord. [3]

And to wait for His Son from heaven, whom He raised from the dead – Jesus. [4]

**I am waiting for the coming
Of the Lord, who died for me;
Oh His words have thrilled my spirit,
"I will come again for thee!"**

———————

[1] *Psalm 39:7* [2] *Psalm 25:3* [3] *Psalm 27:14*
[4] *1 Thessalonians 1:10*

Day Twenty One

Never Forsaken

O Lord, do not forsake me; be not far from me, O my God. [1]

For the Lord will not forsake his people for His great name's sake. [2]

Those who know your name will trust in you, for you, Lord, have never forsaken those who seek you. [3]

God has said, never will I leave you: never will I forsake you. [4]

I will not forget thee or leave thee;
In My hands I'll hold thee, in My arms I'll fold thee;
I will not forget thee or leave thee—
I am thy Redeemer, I will care for thee.

---

[1]Psalm 38:21 [2]1 Samuel 12:22 (AV) [3]Psalm 9:10
[4]Hebrews 13:5

Day Twenty Two

Poverty

Yet I am poor and needy; may the Lord think of me. [1]

Be pleased, O Lord, to save me; O Lord, come quickly to help me. [2]

This poor man called, and the Lord heard him; he saved him out of all his troubles. [3]

Listen, my dear brothers: Has not God chosen those who are poor in the eyes of the world to be rich in faith and to inherit the kingdom?[4]

He did not reign upon a throne of ivory,
But died upon the Cross of Calvary
For sinners there, He counted all He owned but loss,
And he surveyed His kingdom from a cross.

---

[1] Psalm 40:17   [2] Psalm 40:13   [3] Psalm 34:6
[4] James 2:5

Day Twenty Three

Teach me

Teach me your way, O Lord; lead me in a straight path. [1]

Show me your ways, O Lord, teach me your paths; guide me in your truth and teach me. [2]

Teach me, and I will be quiet; Show me where I have been wrong. [3]

For the Holy Spirit will teach you at that time what you should say. [4]

He leadeth me! O blessed thought!
O words with heavenly comfort fraught!
Whate'er I do, Where'er I be,
Still 'tis God's hand that leadeth me.

---

[1]Psalm 27:11 [2]Psalm 25:4, 5 [3]Job 6:24
[4]Luke 12:12

Day Twenty Four

The King

Your eyes will see the king in his beauty and view a land that stretches afar.[1]

We know that when he appears we shall be like him, for we shall see him as he is.[2]

The king is enthralled by your beauty; honour him, for he is your lord.[3]

For the Lord himself will come down from heaven, with a loud command, with the voice of the archangel and with the trumpet call of God.[4]

The bride eyes not her garment,
But her dear Bridegroom's face;
I will not gaze at glory,
But on my King of grace.

---

[1]Isaiah 33:17 [2]1 John 3:2 [3]Psalm 45:11
[4]1 Thessalonians 4:16

Day Twenty Five

God, the Lord

I will give you the treasures of darkness, riches stored in secret places, so that I may know that I am the Lord. [1]

I am the Lord, and there is no other; apart from me there is no God. [2]

And there is no God apart from me, a righteous God and a Saviour; there is none but me. [3]

My Lord and my God. [4]

God everywhere hath sway,
And all things serve His might,
His every act pure blessing is,
His path unsullied light.

---

[1] Isaiah 45:3 [2] Isaiah 45:5 [3] Isaiah 45:21
[4] John 20:28

Day Twenty Six

The God Who Listens

———

Hear us, O our God, for we are despised. [1]

*Answer me when I call to you, O my righteous
God. Give me relief from my distress;
be merciful to me and hear my prayer.* [2]

*Do not hide your face from your servant; answer
me quickly, for I am in trouble.* [3]

Father, I thank you that you have heard me. [4]

> **Prayer is the burden of a sigh,
> The falling of a tear;
> The upward glancing of an eye,
> When none but God is near.**

———

[1] Nehemiah 4:4   [2] Psalm 4:1   [3] Psalm 69:17
[4] John 11:41

Day Twenty Seven

Trials

Do not be surprised at the painful trial you are suffering, as though something strange were happening to you. [1]

These have come so that your faith – of greater worth than gold, which perishes even though refined by fire – may be proved genuine and may result in praise, glory and honour. [2]

God tested Abraham. [3]

I want to test the sincerity of your love. [4]

When through the deep waters I call thee to go,
The floods of distress shall not thee overflow;
For I will be with thee, thy troubles to bless,
And sanctify to thee thy deepest distress.

---

[1] 1 Peter 4:12 [2] 1 Peter 1:7 [3] Genesis 22:1
[4] 2 Corinthians 8:8

Day Twenty Eight

God's Faithfulness

God is faithful, by whom ye were called unto the fellowship of his Son Jesus Christ our Lord. [1]

There hath no temptation taken you but such as is common to man: but God is faithful, who will not suffer you to be tempted above that ye are able. [2]

If we are faithless, he will remain faithful, for he cannot disown himself. [3]

If we confess our sins, he is faithful and just and will forgive us our sins and purify us from all unrighteousness. [4]

God will through eternal ages
Not one sin remember more;
Blotted from the accusing pages
Naught the writing can restore.

---

[1] *1 Corinthians 1:9 (AV)*   [2] *1 Corinthians 10;13 (AV)*
[3] *2 Timothy 2:13*   [4] *1John 1:9*

Day Twenty Nine

The Man Christ Jesus

―――――

Behold, the man! [1]

This man welcomes sinners. [2]

This man has done nothing wrong. [3]

Surely this man was the Son of God! [4]

Will you go with this man? [5]

> **Man of Sorrows! what a name**
> **For the Son of God, who came**
> **Ruined sinners to reclaim.**
> **Hallelujah! what a Saviour!**

―――――

[1] *John 19:5 (AV)*
[2] *Luke 15:2*
[3] *Luke 23:41*
[4] *Mark 15:39*
[5] *Genesis 24:58*

Day Thirty

Grace

My grace is sufficient for you. [1]

And God is able to make all grace abound to you. [2]

From the fulness of his grace we have all received one blessing after another. [3]

Grace and truth came through Jesus Christ. [4]

But by the grace of God I am what I am. [5]

> **Through many dangers, toils and snares,
> I have already come;
> 'Tis grace that brought me safe thus far,
> And grace will lead me home.**

---

[1] *2 Corinthians 12:9* [2] *2 Corinthians 9:8* [3] *John 1:16*
[4] *John 1:17* [5] *1 Corinthians 15:10*

Day Thirty One

Remembrance

O Sovereign Lord, remember me. O God, please strengthen me just once more. [1]

Remember me, O Lord, when you show favour to your people. [2]

Remember me with favour, O my God. [3]

And the Lord listened and heard. A scroll of remembrance was written in his presence concerning those who feared the Lord and honoured his name. [4]

**Can a mother's tender care
Cease toward the child she bare?
Yes, she may forgetful be,
Yet will I remember thee.**

---

[1] Judges 16:28 [2] Psalm 106:4 [3] Nehemiah 13:31
[4] Malachi 3:16

This edition copyright © 1993 Hayes Press

**Published by Hayes Press
Essex Road, Leicester, England LE4 7EE**

Revised Edition 1993

Acknowledgments

Bible quotations from the Holy Bible, New International Version, copyright 1973, 1978, 1984 International Bible Society. Published by Hodder & Stoughton.

Artwork by Elsie B Sands

Printed and bound in England.

This edition copyright © 1993 Hayes Press

**Published by Hayes Press
Essex Road, Leicester, England LE4 7EE**

Revised Edition 1993

Acknowledgments

Bible quotations from the Holy Bible, New International Version, copyright 1973, 1978, 1984 International Bible Society. Published by Hodder & Stoughton.

Artwork by Elsie B Sands

Printed and bound in England.